woodlands

nature~magic~mystery~myth

woodlands

nature~magic~mystery~myth

d. ellis phelps, editor

Moon Shadow Sanctuary Press
Bulverde, Texas

Copyright © 2022
Moon Shadow Sanctuary Press, Bulverde, Texas

Individual poems and photographs are copyrighted by the authors and artists and are used with permission. All rights reserved. No part of this book may be used or reproduced by any means, graphic, electronic, or mechanical, including photocopying, recording, taping or by an information storage retrieval system without the express written permission of the individual writer or photographer except in the case of brief quotations embodied in critical articles and reviews or used as epigraphs in derivative work.

Library of Congress Control Number: 2022922014
ISBN #: 979-8-218-10757-4

Printed in the United States
Moon Shadow Sanctuary Press, Bulverde, Texas
www.moonshadowsanctuarypress.org

Title Poem: *14 Ways to Stay Awake,* Spirit Thom

Cover Art: *Wedding 5,* Cynthia Yachtman

Cover Graphic Design: d. ellis phelps

Interior Layout & Design: d. ellis phelps

The editor gratefully acknowledges the publications in which these works first appeared:

"Camping, Circa 1970," *Of the Forest*
"Emily Dickinson Was More than a White Dress," *Not Me: Poems About Other Women*
"Firewood," *From Every Moment a Second*
"Forest Homage," *Plant People: An Anthology of Environmental Artists*
"In a Moment of Existential Anxiety, Kermit Plays the Banjo," *MockingHeart Review*
"Love Poem," *Of the Forest*
"Lyme Ticks and Ladybugs," *Strange Company*
"Ruffled," *Vita Brevis*
"This Oak," *Slippery Elm*
"Vernal Reach," *the after: poems only a planet could love*

Contents

Leslie Soule — 2
Foreword: The Sacredness of Trees — 2

ARPEGGIO — 8

Stephanie L. Harper — 9
American Beech — 9

Tristan Franz — 10
One (Jamaica bay Wildlife Refuge) — 10

Susan Coultrap-McQuin — 11
Cathedral Calls — 11

Victoria Costello — 12
Connection — 12

Victoria Costello — 14
Joshua Tree — 14

Brigid Cooley — 15
summer lullaby — 15

Lorena Caputo — 16
Spirit Suite—Ètude N° 11 — 16

Linda Ferguson — 18
Campling Circa 1970 — 18

Alice Campbell Romano — 19
Jacaranda Tree, Los Angeles — 19

Sandi Stromberg — 20
The Wood Thrush in July — 20

Lynne Burnett   21
    Greenway Sound Swallows   21

Alex Angeline   22
    Birdsong   22

Lynne Burnett   23
    Note to a Friend   23

Liam Wilson   24
    Vernal Reach   24

Melissa Wold   25
    Spirals of Immortality   25

GHOST WALK   28

Mary Chapman   29
    weeping women   29

RC deWinter   32
    Ghost Walk   32

Jenny Wrenn   33
    Embrace   33

RC deWinter   34
    After Africa   34

Julie Corpus   35
    Strange Hibernations   35

Kendra Preston Leonard   36
    Ghost Jam   36

Sharon Mitchell   37
    Ursus Mater   37

Ruth McArthur	**38**
Rapture	38

CONTINUE TO CURVE — 40

Julie Martin	**41**
Marvel	41
Julie Martin	**42**
Forest Homage	42
Joan Leotta	**43**
Ruffled	43
Karla Linn Merrifield	**44**
First-name Basis	44
Jean Ryan	**46**
Editor's Choice Award	**46**
Lichen	46
Robert Okaji	**47**
This Oak	47
Robert Okaji	**48**
Firewood	48
Kendra Preston Leonard	**49**
I. She Calls it a Fairy Tree	49
Wendy Dunmeyer	**52**
Ranunculus	52
Wendy Carlisle	**54**
Toads	54
Robert Okaji	**55**

In a Moment of Existential Anxiety,	55
Kermit Plays the Banjo	55

M. Lynne Squires — 56
Trees Speak — 56

Lorena Caputo — 57
Talking Trees — 57

THE WANTING SILENCE — 58

Bernard Jacobson — 59
The Hills the Spirits Hold — 59

Linda Ferguson — 61
Emily Dickinson Was More Than a White Dress — 61

Maria Illich — 62
Night Vision — 62

Sharon Mitchell — 66
Spirit Lake — 66

Linda Ferguson — 68
Love Poem — 68

Jennifer Lagier — 69
In the Mansion of Stars — 69

Sterling Warner — 70
Beguiling — 70

Kerfe Roig — 71
Harvest Moon — 71

Krissi Stocks — 72
On Assignment in Harbour Grace — 72

Annie Snider	**75**
Observation	75
Charles Darnell	**76**
Mushrooms	76
Victoria Dym	**77**
Fruitbody	77
Cynthia Bernard	**78**
Mycelia	78
Lorena Caputo	**80**
Roots	80

PURE ARCHITECTURE 82

Jean Ryan	**83**
Lyme Ticks and Ladybugs	83
Karla Linn Merrifield	**87**
Organic Tanka	87
Greg Illich	**88**
In a Fading Time	88
Ann Calandro	**90**
Before the Soup	90
Paul Gutting	**91**
Daylight Savings	91
Paul Gutting	**92**
D. C. al Fine	92
Charles Darnell	**94**
Crysalis	94

Cynthia Bernard	**96**
Weathered Wood	96

REACHING FOR THE FAUN — 98

M. C. Aster	**99**
Afternoon Lights	99
Chelsea Grieve	**100**
dream of tir-na-nog*	100
M. C. Aster	**102**
The Old Toll Bridge	102
Sharon Mitchell	**105**
The Naiad's Dream *	105
M. C. Aster	**106**
The Mavka at Midnight*	106
Wendy Dunmeyer	**107**
Eridanus*	107
Wendy Dunmeyer	**108**
selene, to pandia*	108
Paul Gutting	**110**
Calling the Wild	110

NEW VOLTAIRES — 112

Ann Howells	**113**
Welcome Morning	113
Ann Howells	**114**
Day of the Dragonflies	114
Kendra Preston Leonard	**115**

Replenish	115
Mobi Warren	**116**
Diadasia Bee Asleep in a White Prickly Poppy	116
Alice Campbell Romano	**117**
It Never Rains in Los Angeles	117
Chris Billings	**118**
Skinny Dipping	118
Alice Campbell Romano	**120**
Gods of a Hudson River Storm	120
Chris Billings	**121**
The Nelipot Way	121
Spirit Thom	**123**
14 Ways to Stay Awake	123

BIOGRAPHIES 124

for trees & those who love them

Leslie Soule

Foreword: The Sacredness of Trees

Human reverence for trees seems to go back as far as our mutual existence. Whatever the source of our deep connectedness, the cliché has an element of truth to it: if we love nature, trees are the first element of it that we might want to hug. [1].

The term "tree hugger" has been applied to hippies and environmentalists alike, and some see it as a teasing, derogatory term while others embrace the title. But the idea is far from a modern concept. *Tree worship, known as dendrolatry, refers to the tendency of societies throughout history to worship and mythologize trees. Trees play an important role in many mythologies and religions. They have been given deep meaning through the ages.* [2].
There are many myths surrounding trees: One of them, is of the dryads of Greek mythology who were always female nymphs connected to a particular tree. The hamadryads were so connected to their trees that if their tree died, they did as well.

As humans, we witness leaves fall from deciduous trees and anticipate their spring revival, seeing them as powerful symbols of growth, death, and rebirth.

I once saw a *Shoe Tree* in California, upon which people had thrown all sorts of pairs of shoes, with the shoelaces tied together. I didn't know how this had come to be, but something about that tree was mesmerizing. I pulled off the side of the road, gazed at it for a few minutes, and then took an old pair of shoes from the back of the car. After tying the shoelaces together, I threw them up there as well. *The shoe tree blooms with polymer beauty. A work of art like this may last for generations, tracing our history by our sneakers...as long as the tree doesn't die or get attacked by shoe tree murderers.*[3] But this cultural phenomenon may tie itself to the age-old tradition of "wishing trees" where wreaths and ribbons are hung on trees for good luck.

In the Norse myth of *Sigurd the Volsung*, an old man (whom we assume to be Odin), takes a sword and thrusts it into a tree. The similarity between this myth and that of King Arthur pulling his sword from the stone, is noteworthy. Like King Arthur, Sigurd is the only one who can pull this enchanted sword free. In Norse mythology, this tree is known as Barnstokker. But perhaps the most well-known tree in Norse mythology, is the world tree, called Yggdrasil. It was from this tree, that Odin hung upside-down for nine days in order to gain the magic of the runes. Also, in Norse mythology, man was to have been created from an ash tree, while women were created from an elm tree.

In the mythos created by J.R.R. Tolkien, two trees also figure prominently, as these are the *Two Trees of Valinor*, one gold and one silver, known as Laurelin and Telperion.

In Roman mythology, Silvanus was the god of the woods and protector of the forest. He has associations with Mars, the Roman god of war, and was thus thought to be the giver of the art of forest warfare. Sacrifices given to Silvanus included grapes, ears of corn, milk, meat, wine, and pigs.

In Britain, there is the legend of the Glastonbury Thorn, which was said to have grown miraculously from the staff of Joseph of Arimathea, when he thrust it into the ground. The blooming of the Glastonbury Thorn is seen as a mark of divine favor.

In the book *Three Gold Pieces*, which is a Greek folk tale, a tree figures prominently as well, as there is a Moor who sticks gold pieces to the leaves of a tree. The main character, who realizes that whatever the Moor is up to is none of his business, does not stop to ask what is going on, and ends up being rewarded for following this course of action.

Since ancient days trees have been used to represent life, growth, wisdom, prosperity and more in legends, poetry, literature, and religion. We all know the symbolism behind an olive branch and the Tree of Knowledge from the Garden of Eden [4]

The Living Urn company offers a tree and nutrient system that combines with the ashes of a deceased person to provide life to a tree. This is a powerful symbol of renewal, and shows how connected we are to trees, both physically and symbolically.

Mystical and majestic, trees are seen as ancient living beings. From healing to protection, trees have played a large role in our history. Cultures have coveted their energy and worshipped them. Providing us with so many of our basic needs, trees offer us far more with their mystical connection to us spiritually. A great energy and a wisdom are believed to flow through them. Tree burials and tree memorials have also been a part of mankind dating back centuries [5].

The familiar image known as the *Tree of Life*, shows a tree above the ground and below the ground. The *Field Guide to Trees of North America* [6] tells us that, *A tree's roots form a branching network roughly equal to the tree's crown.* The *Tree of Life* image symbolizes the

interconnectedness of all things, with the branches reaching up to the heavens and the roots delving into the Earth.
As the source of much of the planet's oxygen and thus an important part of Earth's biosphere, as living beings of worship, as healers, as shade-givers, as friends, even, let us treat these majestic tree-beings with the deep respect and reverence they are due.

1. National Wildlife Federation, https://www.nwf.org/
2. The Living Urn, https://www.thelivingurn.com/
3. Roadside America, https://www.roadsideamerica.com/search/tip
4. Augustine Nursery Blog, https://augustinenursery.com/the-symbolic-meanings-of-trees/
5. The Living Urn, https://www.thelivingurn.com/
6. *National Wildlife Federation Field Guide to Trees of North America.* Kershner, Bruce (2008) Union Square & Co., Pub.

...And I cannot teach you the prayer of the seas and the forests and the mountains. But you who are born of the mountains and the forests and the seas can find their prayer in your heart...

~Kahlil Gibran

arpeggio

Stephanie L. Harper

American Beech

Let's try, here,
in the cloud-grey
of this centuries-old beech—
stunning Bathsheba,

her toes, immense,
clinging to the path's edge—
to be held
tightly enough;

let's try, in this world
feathered green,
its daylight's golden
crowns & rosy breasts,

its predawn depths
teeming with robin-songs,
to dream ourselves
being alive:

Shouldn't we try
to wake up
high in this tree,
in tranquil forest-scent,

roll over, lean
the other cheek against her
smooth-muscled wood
& listen?

Tristan Franz

One (Jamaica bay Wildlife Refuge)

I will do one thing with purpose today
one thing informed by the soft crush
of soil and leaf, one thing
in response to the call of gulls
the tempered ripple of a marsh tide
today I will be one thing
that glides with the gliding
that rustles with the rustling

I'll be here on a bench, free-soloing this moment
serene and satisfied
with the center of things, the singular
of plural — I'll be a collective noun
a word encompassing all
the wildlife here — myself included
a sound like the one in the distance
like the gulls' constant chant at us all
one, one
I'll be one

Susan Coultrap-McQuin

Cathedral Calls

I enter the primal forest,
its golden carpet laid down,
its pillars of trees wide open
to parables in the sky.

Above me, a litany resounds
with amen from birds in the choir.
The incense of soil surrounds me.
I sink to my seat on the ground.

Leaves whisper and nod in welcome,
invite me to join the call,
add my voice to the earthy hymns,
my heart to this ancient soul.

Victoria Costello

Connection

Sunny leaned against a massive boulder, winded, her side aching, happy to surrender her weight to its smooth heft. After an hour of hiking, she was surprised her sixty-nine-year-old body had made it this far. A minor miracle occurred that morning when a small voice raised her to brave the summer weekend traffic and lingering wildfire smoke to come, alone, to this desert trail near Lone Pine. An old haunt.

With her pupils narrowed to slits, Sunny surveyed the grove of otherworldly Joshua Trees, the glorious payoff at trail's end that had drawn her back here. She'd long marveled at this largest of the yucca plant for its audacious reach and stark beauty in such inhospitable surroundings. She rested her gaze on a big mama some twenty feet away and heard a feint buzz. As if by accident, a feedback loop materialized between her and this tree. Its spiny branches turned into arms and multiplied, Shiva-like, thrashing and writhing. As the buzz got louder, a surge of current reached Sunny's lower body, igniting pinpricks as the current tried to move up her legs and thighs. Sunny pictured uneven pavement and a road crew using a jackhammer to remove old, cracked cement and cried out first in pain, then frustration as she took in the sad state of her core, too weak to accept the gift being offered.

Concentrating on her breath, she inhaled the fragrance emanating from the Dragon blood sagebrush that carpeted the desert floor, hoping the pungent aroma from its tiny red blossoms would open her other senses. She conjured a child staring through bakery glass at an iced cupcake, an ingenue catching her breath when the boy of her dreams glanced in her direction, the scholar she used to be immersed in the medieval texts that had given her entry to an enchanted world. Desire became desperation and her rattled mind dispensed bread crumbs: Unus mundus. Jung's scarab. The proto consciousness of organic matter. Spooky action at a distance. Wave. Particle. Observer. Observed. But which was she?

    She considered the mama Joshua tree anew and remembered she was both. She put a hand on her solar plexus and detected a feint current. Feeling emboldened, she gave her attention over to the teaming community of nocturnal creatures who dwelled beneath her feet. Lizard, kangaroo rat, badger, gopher, kit fox. She formed the intention to release her individuality, allowing the borders of her skin and bones to dissolve into an endlessly repeating fractal, the essence of Sunny as a recursive, self-repeating pattern joining with the other beings who dwelled in this place to form a chain, a dynamic representation of chaos at peace with itself. Here were the voices of the plant, animal, and mineral life-forms around her. The air aflutter in the wake of a swarm of Painted Ladies. Yucca needles vibrating like the strings of a violin. Baritone notes echoed from the boulders, together wisps of ethereal harmony vacillating with the wind, coming in and out of a frequency her ears could receive.

    Part way down the mountain, Sunny sat on a rock to take a drink and wondered what she'd done to deserve the exquisite sense of connection that remained a palpable vibration coursing through her limbs. On the tail end of a songbird's call, she thought she heard, *Nothing. Absolutely nothing.* To which she laughed and whispered:

    Thank you.

    She rearranged her backpack and started down again, careful not to trip over a pile of fallen rocks blocking the trail. In response to a woodpecker's insistent squawk, she looked to the east, where shifting winds had parted the sooty cloudbank to reveal the majestic summit of Mount Whitney. *My god*! She'd forgotten it was there.

Victoria Costello

Joshua Tree

Brigid Cooley

summer lullaby

sweat pools on my collarbone
sunburnt skin under a bright july sky
& picnic blankets spread across brown grass
i am just another park goer
looking for solace here in the shade
leaves rustle overhead
disturbed by feverish winds
and something i don't quite have words for
begins to swell inside me
memories long forgotten:
my ex lover
gingerly pressing piano keys
composing a masterpiece
all while i
hum a melancholic lullaby
& turn a dog-eared page

Lorena Caputo

Spirit Suite—Ètude Nº 11

On the back acreage, foot-deep ashes bed the fire pit. Charred wood speckles the grey like the black spots of a wizened jaguar.

Yesterday I walked down there. I sat on a sycamore log for a longest while. I felt the Earth's calling to stretch upon her green tender-herb blanket.

& there I laid, head turned South, resting upon crossed arms. My solar plexus, the umbilical of my silver cord rooting deep into the rich spring soil. The cool breeze stroked my bare forearms.

& I jerked into this-world consciousness with the nip of every insect. & floated back … standing on the rim of that Other World. & I jerked into this-world wakefulness with the sounds of a large cat walking through the wild grains. Nothing was there, time & again, visible to this world's eye. Finally, I accepted the presence of jaguar.

I focused upon my breathing, drawing it into & beyond my heart & my throat where, unwittingly, unknowingly, I had been stopping it … not wanting to touch that still-tender wound.

My breath of Life stung it with the realization of lessons yet to be learned.

The backdoor slam flapped past the outbuildings, across the already calf-high grasses. I heard my name called.

& I jumped off that brink & sank into the depths of the Other World.

After a long while of the sun-warmth seeping into my body, melting away scabs I'd formed, I awoke bathed in sweat where skin touched skin. Toxins oozing from my mouth in thin rivulets.

I slowly raised my body from Mother's embrace, seeing the Light surrounding her & All Relations, & feeling my heart once more, the scaly crust stripped away. & I knew, even more, that my healing was growing & forming.

I looked at where my head-on-arms had lain: there, a four-leaf clover, its new-born leaves large in the mid-afternoon sun.

In these front-acre trees to my right, I hear a snap. I look up from this pen. A bluebird alights, body clear blue, breast serene orange.

& I remember back to when I was only five or six. In that old brown-stone castlette, I would always ask the librarian for the picture of that bird from her file. & for hours I would behold that precious summer sky, brilliant summer sunset in my child's hands.

Linda Ferguson

Campling Circa 1970

My chocolate-eyed brother croons to me
from his sleeping bag.

Sprinkle of pine needles on the roof of our blue tent.
Canvas walls a lullaby cradling the ghost
of marshmallow smoke.

Eyes closed, I see a cinnamon tree stump perched on the
hill beyond.

My brother says the stump is a small bear.

I want it to be a bear. I want to rest my cheek against the
bear's side and feel his warm ribs rising.

I want to hold all the bear's sighs in my arms.

I want him to sing to me all my life.

Alice Campbell Romano

Jacaranda Tree, Los Angeles

On the lawn yesterday in full blossom, Tree, you were a
giant, lavender-blue party balloon in the shape of a brain,
your trunk the brain stem, your limbs tucked out of sight.

Rain—rare visitor—paid a call in the night.
This morning, across our taffeta-green lawn,
bows on a Victorian dress, your lost petals lay.

Your trunk is rough, scaled. Your branches thin
to bare, bent twigs, your fronds too scant to cover you.
A tree has no coy hands to disguise her nakedness.

Your skin was once so smooth. At fourteen, you put out
your first blossoms. You could be fifty now, or seventy:
your bark already thickening when we moved in.

Your bell flowers—sticky—even smell like honey.
Angelinos know never to park under a Jacaranda.
The blossoms on the lawn begin to shrivel. I must

remember to cut the neighbor's ivy at the base
of your trunk, end its insidious climb. It pushes
into your cracked skin, grows arrogant leaves

while you lose yours, creeps up your boughs
to steal light at your canopy. This cannot happen.
Take in sunshine for as long as we both are here.

Change the air below you when you are in full bloom.
Make this harsh light subtle, faintly blue,
sweet with your own perfume.

Sandi Stromberg

The Wood Thrush in July

All winter I heard him
peck the glass,
disappearing
when I opened the blinds,
a scurry in the red-tip photinia,
a tentative tick of claws,
a wing flick in the scarlet leaves
of the Chinese maple.
Now that the air is heavy
with deep summer,
I thought him gone,
following his mystical map
back to the north,
a harbinger of spring
to wintry climes.
But no. That soft tick clicks
my windowpane.
Through the slats
I spy him perched
on the narrow sill,
his brown-speckled breast
throbbing. He cocks
his quizzical head at me.
I tilt mine, too, pondering
what is written:
For man knoweth not his time,
as the birds that are caught
in the snare.
We hold each other
motionless, mesmerized
by the mysterious
order in these things.

Lynne Burnett

Greenway Sound Swallows

At the juncture of two red-carpeted docks,
under the eaves of a floating restaurant:
a nest, four years in the making—
continually revised, like a poem
still trying to say what it must say
to survive an awkward beginning.

There, two swallows attend to their secret:
when one arrives, the other leaves,
each in turn spreading wings and zooming,
twittering through the dazzled August hours
we share, disturbing the moss-curtained trees
for tidbits of insect and fluff.

In their tidal dance of coming and going,
in the loyal, immediate beak rub — is an
instinct or need, that I would call vision,
pursued in a tireless song of wings and
this I lie down with, after the sun has set.

I sleep in the darkness of what is not mine
to see. Life ripens in that dark, and in
the crack between our worlds
comes a day longed for, its light
effulgent, easing in.

Alex Angeline

Birdsong

in the wooz of wake
into Summer's swelt
I dune the grinds
I pour the milk

I fraction afloat
from ever to is
I am not still space
I am not yet this

enpaused and enplumed
in a Southern cloche
chirrs chorus the lip
of this held exist

Lynne Burnett

Note to a Friend

In the fern's unfurling,
a frond of the life that lives me
frolics in your deep grasses.
Bound to the same sweet earth,
we are bound as well
by the whorl of dreams
that first made us friends.

Some say the coming of rains
and of shadows multiplies
sorrow, but those are the humoured
losses of a protean force
which stretches my green wings
in the variable light
and fires your impressionable
footsteps with purpose.

We move, blade and feather,
in a moist world shared
with an impeccable sense
of the rightness of things—
how firmly this holds
the inner ladder we climb,
one rung apart
from the love that made us.

Liam Wilson

Vernal Reach

Melissa Wold

If by chance I have omitted anything more or less proper or necessary, I beg forgiveness since there is no one who is without fault and circumspect in all matters.

~Leonardo Fibonacci

Spirals of Immortality

We are God's fingerprint
replicated, extrapolated.
Whorls, the world's glint.
Diversity stellated
through a shell in the Aegean Sea.
Spirals speak of immortality

replicated, extrapolated.
Patterns form galaxies.
Independent, interdependent atoms pulsated
creating truths and fallacies.
Enmeshed within the cosmic web
scrabbling to shore with sea's ebb.

Whorls, the world's glint
reflected in chameleon's tail;
echoed in sunflower's blueprint.
Snail slimes a traceable trail
of molecules defined,
refined to a portrait yet unsigned.

Diversity stellated
into cones, eggs, honeybees.
Stardust-energy migrated,
becoming you, them, me.
Circling through the byzantine,
following ancient rhyme.

Through a shell in the Aegean Sea
kaleidoscope-hues of blue, green, lavender
refract through to eternity.
A nothingness scavenger
determines galactic vectors,
secrete impulsive effectors.

Spirals speak of immortality
in Stephan's Quintet of ghost lyrics.
Rhythmic, vertical loops of infinity
inspire notes of panegyrics.
Perfection of the golden ratio.
Nature's orchestral arpeggio.

ghost walk

Mary Chapman

weeping women

They say I am a woman.   consumed

weeping, whimpering, sniveling, sobbing

with grief. or hate
 or — and this one is my favorite: revenge.

screeching, squalling, clamoring, screaming

You think you know my story.

You warn your children and give yourself
gooseflesh when you whisper *La Llorona* in the dark.

That is not my name.

yelling, bellowing, hollering, crying

 They say I never stop mourning the loss of my children.
easy enough to understand
ask any townswoman of my time. we've all lost. many

see their little grave markers lined up.   row upon row

moaning, whimpering, sobbing, wailing

so, why my story? A mournful mother is nothing new.

sobbing, bawling, sniveling, mewling

29

In some tellings I killed them myself.   Again, I ask – what would be the point?
Purgatory in exchange for soiled diapers? No.

yelling, calling, bleating, squawking

In some versions — the cruelest ones — my husband killed my babies (and then me)

Fine then, revenge.
 This white hot heat is known to many of us
when husband eyes roam.
So, to sanction his lust by removing the nag
and hellions in one go?
That is stupidity, not revenge.

screaming, roaring, shouting, yelling

well. if I am going to be a ghost story,
so be it

but at least let me make it clear
 I am just like you

and her   and her

back and back and back

we are all the same
disregarded, discarded

see the deluge
of untold stories
from decamillennia of women
float soundlessly downriver
forgotten

My story is their story.
I will be their battle cry.

hollering, clamoring, shouting, roaring

at night
under a new moon
when you see a glimmer of white lace
and hear a unearthly cry
It is not me.

It is you.

Or your wife.
Or your daughter.

Yo no soy La Llorona.

RC deWinter

Ghost Walk

Last night you walked, a ghost wrapped in a shroud,
Haunting my dreams through all the endless night.
On seeing you, I called your name aloud;
you glided on, silently recondite.

I followed as you led, not knowing where
you took me, but never was I afraid.
And to the willow grove we did repair,
the one where as a child you had played.

There, throwing off the shroud, you blazed with light;
the moon's bright shining paled in your glow.
You took my hand in yours and said "Good night,
I miss you but it's time for me to go."

Oh come again, and hold my hand once more,
That I may be with you beyond death's door.

Jenny Wrenn

Embrace

Out in these sparse pinon juniper woods
on a rise between arroyos and far from any
narrow black snake of running water

grows a crone of a juniper several hundred
years old her trunk deeply scored and scarred
yet still green along her gnarled gray extremities

in those ancient arms she holds tight a massive trunk
of another tree who grew ages ago by her side
now rootless dangling in her still aching embrace

once I stood very still at the cusp of a winter's dawn
and heard her keening grief along the edge of the breeze
and felt her eternal tears in the fall of frozen sleet

we pine for so romantic and everlasting a love
but I for one can only imagine the erosive agony
of being unable to let go of even your lover's bones

RC deWinter

After Africa

When the Eater of Souls swallowed yours I became
the leftover piece of a puzzle we could never finish.

Head empty of all but dreams.
Heart empty of all but ghosts.
Hands empty of all but words fading to the dust
    of once upon a time.

With an ancient strand of stray elegance
    wound into my DNA
I live in the genteel poverty of the overeducated poor
    – the place where
you buy real maple syrup and good liquor and
    eat less to pay for it.

This is no hardship. Poverty and I are old friends.
But walking this empty corridor into the long goodnight
without you is unacceptable.

Last night I thought I heard the owl call my name,
    but it was
only the rub of a stray branch stuttering in the wind. Pity.
My soul's on the menu whenever Kikiyaon
    needs a midnight snack.

Julie Corpus

Strange Hibernations

Suddenly it's November, and everything's hushed.
The wood frog seeks refuge, then slows
Its heartbeat to await spring's sunlight.
What a bright idea by that tiny creature
To fake his own death.
In a towering house, a widow imprisons herself.
She refuses to eat, only sips water. The widow
Commands her lungs to regulate their breathing
So that winter dreaming can begin in earnest.
This is her grand plan to avoid missing him.
The unbearable hurt tears at her heartstrings.
She cannot go on.

If someone comes looking, they won't
Ever find her: Retama, mesquite, cacti,
And a tall Anacua will impede their progress.
She has made it impossible to trespass her fortress.
Absence matters here.
Her void is a temple, scented like the ocean.
A constant chilly breeze seeping through the cracks,
Fails to disturb her. Neither does the vine which
Ensnares her ankles, laden with green lizards and
Shiny, winged insects.

Suddenly, it's March, and two different hearts
Resume their respective rhythms. In the widow's
House, a hum of shrill creatures rains softly around her.
She's feeling quite different—buoyant.
Her strange hibernation is a success.
She will never know that her grief now resides
In a wood frog's body.

Kendra Preston Leonard

Ghost Jam

Collect the ghosts who are willing.
None of the shouting, or gory:
they disturb the process.
Make them warm with steam
in a kitchen full of silver,
and stir them down
with sugar and agar.

Keep your ghost jam in small jars;
they like to be dispersed as gifts
with a wooden knife and a loaf
of wheat or rye.

Spread the jam on bread;
it is excellent with added hot peppers.
Do not allow your pets
to eat the ghost jam; it is,
however,
safe for horses.

Ghost jam might make you cry,
or it might make you laugh or growl
all the way down the street and into the library.
It might help you sleep, keep your legs quiet,
or give your toddlers headaches.
It is always unpredictable.
Eat it slowly, or fast, for the ghosts
do not care,
warm and sugared and gone.

Sharon Mitchell

Ursus Mater

I took my sorrow
to the mountains.
I struggled under its weight,
my legs weary, my footing unsure.

I went alone,
to find a hidden waterfall.
It was midsummer,
the trail obscured
in waist-high weeds.

I was loathe to turn back,
and loathe to move forward,
stubbornness my only power.
The trail turned to muck
as I slogged uphill, despairing.

Then I saw a bear track, fresh,
in the mud. I looked up.
I could see the waterfall
through the trees. I sent
a prayer of thanks to the bear.
Only the animals know
the way to the Healing Waters.

Ruth McArthur

Rapture

With a graceless
    lunge
        she returns
            to muddy waters.

        Homemade bra, panties worn
            with age, majestic
                stomach a convex wonder.

            Her hands are stars,
                smile an invitation,
                    eyes innocent as a child's.

                Spirit of Bliss,
                    she arose from mud
                        to teach us joy.

continue to curve

Julie Martin

Marvel

Stoked, hopped up on sugar sauce,
they poke their freaky, flicky
tongues in one thousand flowers each day.

Knights-in-shining-armor,
these flying jewels pierce the air,
gorgets aglint in the sun.

Less like Tinkerbell, more like Jaws,
open up wide like a catcher's mitt
and prey on mosquitoes and gnats.

Little bad asses
inhabit a realm nearly invisible to humans—
all we get is a glimpse,

of a whirling psychedelic blur.
Yet they possess Super Powers— see colors
we can't perceive, off the spectrum.

Hummer Warz —they spin into aerial dogfights,
use their bills to fence and spar,
pluck feathers, defend territory.

They've got the moves,
twists, turns, maneuvers,
steep dives at break-neck speeds,

not afraid to embrace the dark side.

Julie Martin

Forest Homage

Walk amongst the tamarack trees—
knobby spurs of vivid green,
brush like tufts, tightly clumped, conceal
the understory, yet there are telltale
signs that porcupines have gnawed through
the tough outer edges of bark

like outdated beliefs, peeled away,
uncovering what is fresh and tender.
Continue to curve along this trail
of leaf litter, with occasional rocks and
sphagnum moss while layers of soft mud
kiss the lug soles of leather boots.

Dark clouds bruise the sky's azure-blue
but this perfect day will not be ruined
for, below, birds rustle and forage in flocks
shuffling on the loose ground
and, above, the white-throated sparrow's song
cuts an opening through the woods.

Joan Leotta

Ruffled

Ambling about in mid-morn's quiet
on a small gravel drive carved out
between two rows of loblolly pine,
my meandering reverie is broken by
a flash of feather—
white, black, capped with crimson.
He darts by closely—my cheek's
warmed by his wing in passing.
Ruffled now, roused from reverie,
my eye follows his flight to a
refuge high in clustered pine needles.
Only his red feathers show now.
Tat, tat, tat—he's at work
finding lunch in the bark,
I return to my well-worn path,
refreshed, invigorated by the flash of
beauty that crossed my path this morning,
grateful for the break in routine,
for a moment of being ruffled, a
close connection with an other.

Karla Linn Merrifield

First-name Basis

I knew a Tree-Spirit named Roger who once wore
a palm-frond crown in Zanzibar, but more often
listened intently

to the soughing of wind through longleaf pines, the rattle
of squirrels acrobatting among myrtles
in southeastern American climes,

and pond cypress in stillness following boardwalks of
dendrology—
himself traveling in snaking tracks on trunks and limbs

through sloughs and swamps and up
and over beach swales;
I frequently also witnessed him threading the bare-naked
Standing Ones

of forest cemeteries of barrier islands, Jekyll, Hunting,
Cayo Costa, Lovers Key,
so many others in southern Atlantic Ocean,
in Gulf of Mexico;

On one occasion I know firsthand how he held a tete-à-tete,
canopy-à-canopy,
with General Sherman Sequoia
in the Sierra Nevada of California,

and tangled his thoughts in the prop roots
of mangrove trees at the fringes
of earth and the seventh sea of Belize;

he made himself understood to ancient bristlecones
whose songs with him
were lentissimo above ten thousand feet above sea level
in Utah's Cedar Breaks;

and he frequently spoke Live Oak fluently,
often discussing their pleasure
in hosting Spanish moss (*properly an epiphyte*,
he'd nit-pick we Two-Leggeds)

and resurrection ferns up massive columns
and along the sprawling
heavy timbers of a queenly species he adored,

including the champion he encountered
in LaCrosse, Florida,
who shared her secret of longevity:

Stand tall until it is time to fall aground,
decompose, be nurse log;
a pileated woodpecker shall one day
appreciate your hospitality.

Jean Ryan
Editor's Choice Award

Lichen

Bonded to a boulder,
living on air and random rain,
a forty-year-old lichen
claims a thumbprint of space.
Centuries from now it will be
the size of a dinner plate,
will still be young
when the millennium turns—
not that age applies
to a thing designed to override death.
Maybe this doesn't sound
like much of a life:
stuck on stone, nothing to do
but make more crust.
Or maybe it's a thrill a minute,
living up to all that potential.
I would like to find out:
to lie on a sun-warmed rock
and give myself up,
to become with steady assurance
all I was ever meant to be.

Robert Okaji

This Oak

Never rooted in Tibet,
has not watched a whale breach
a November Pacific dusk, or guzzled
bitter beer near Vesuvius. Nor has it
absorbed the warmth of a loved one's
hip on a frozen morning long after
the embers' glow has greyed
and the windows blossomed
white. It cannot know the beauty
of disparate instruments playing
in joyous harmony. It will whisper
no incantations, does not smile,
won't ever feel the anticipation
of a first kiss after a complicated
courtship. The bouquets of Bordeaux
elude it, as do tears or the benefits
of laughter. Why, then, do I envy it so?

Robert Okaji

Firewood

For two years the oak
loomed, leafless.
We had aged
together, but somehow
I survived the drought
and ice storms, the
regret and wilt,
the explosions within,
and it did not.

I do not know
the rituals of trees,
how they mourn
a passing, or if
the sighs I hear
betray only my own
frailties, but even
as I fuel the saw and
tighten the chain,
I look carefully
for new growth.

Kendra Preston Leonard

~inspired by photographs by Angela Wagner

I. She Calls it a Fairy Tree

Let me slip
into that beautiful space
where the tree meets the ground,
that entrance, shallow-seeming,
to an arboreal world,
fantastic, unknown.
If I just turn my shoulders,
I will pass through the twin arms of bark
and trunk
into
into that warm
dark
space,
and through,
into
an elsewhere.

The tree promises a caress
as I pass
and inside
I will find earth and air,
chlorophyll
that is the green headiness
of the new
rise up through the center
arms into branches thick
and fine and leafy

and I will abide,
pleasure-full.

II.   What Spenser Gave

I stand in the grove, copper-lit,
and refuse false dreams and the
dragon of despair.
Let me now be
cloudily enwrapped
in gentle ease.

Come with me
to this
place that is hushed,
a gentle bower touching moss and vine.

See the boar and her hoglets,
fierce machines on tiny legs.
Hear the leaves telling stories,
reciting names and spells.

Weasel and pheasant,
partridge and hare
process before us;
but take my hand
and walk with me
to where the water
slides in time over rock.

III.   *Cornus florida*

Hound-berries on the dog-tree,
drupes, dinner for cardinals,
all red and white:
blood and allegory
inevitably follow

where branches break
or leaves fall, trampled by
boots and shoes.

Here the branch is curved,
sufficient
to hold
a child and her book

before the engladed waterfalls
call her away,
shadier
enchantments
surround

the dragonfly
and where the frog sings
to the trout.

Wendy Dunmeyer

~for Allison

Ranunculus

A bronze frog sits near
the shallow fresh-water pond
and from the moss sings
to katydid acoustics
his baritone aria,

the tale of a boy
who, dressed in green and gold silks,
played in the forest
all day long and sang until
the canopy echoed back

his trilled treble notes.
One day, the woodland dryads,
startled by the noise,
fell from their shaded branches
high in the oak and ash trees.

So the shy dryads
followed the echoes' return
to the boy and breathed
a spell that changed him into
a green-leafed, bright gold flower,

a flower that blooms
each spring near the shallow pond
where the bronze frog sings
to katydid acoustics
his baritone aria.

Wendy Carlisle

Toads

The endangered Wyoming
the slender Dwarf

the red-spotted Canadian
red striped Burrowing

the Cliff Chirping
Greenhouse, Four-digit
the Vietnamese, Natterjack

Cane toad
toxic, appetitive, fecund

the African Tree
tiny, viviparous—

all Bufonidae, true toads
toothless, sticky tongued,
dry skinned, bumpy

only the Golden Toad, now extinct—
was smooth and bright

Robert Okaji

**In a Moment of Existential Anxiety,
Kermit Plays the Banjo**

If there is no one to hear,
where do the sounds
hide, when do they die? All this
and a greater unknowing, a hollowed,
regretful stump. That plop. And whose
voice is ever heard? Which darkness
weaves into space, sputtering
among stars into more
emptiness, spilling into
the deep black, becoming
a greater zero? He ponders
the difficulties of greenness,
considers rainbows, looks up,
plucks the strings, sings his song.

M. Lynne Squires

Trees Speak

If a tree speaks in the forest, does anyone hear it? Yes, the surrounding trees rustle in response. Nearby animals understand the quiet, near-silent language of trees. The brush of the branches against other trees — a hug, a touch. The swaying of trees is the waltz of the woods. Birds and squirrels ride along, not unlike a child dancing on top of her father's shoes.

Trees enjoy a synergetic life with the weather. The wind blows and the trees dance. The sun shines and the forest reaches farther toward the sky. Skies darken and leaves turn their faces to the ground, hiding from the pelting raindrops soon to come. Storms thrash and throw the weaker branches crashing to the ground. Lightening both illuminates and tears down. Younger trees bend and sway. Older, hardened trees sometimes succumb and fall. Still, they speak from the forest floor, their usefulness merely changing shape.

Trees are reincarnated. Seeds turn to sprouts, sprouts to seedlings, and seedlings to saplings. Fallen comrades rot and decompose, but their usefulness is not over. They nurture the seeds in the cocoon of their composting arms. They whisper to the youngsters just taking root.

Trees speak, and we all listen. Sometimes we reject what they have to say. We curse the fallen. We gather those scattered about, to use, to burn. But when we choose to listen, we learn from the quiet sentries of the earth.

Lorena Caputo

Talking Trees

the wanting silence

Bernard Jacobson

The Hills the Spirits Hold

In rarer moments, when I glimpse beyond
The wanting silence of my mind
I leave myself in search of sacred sighs
Amongst the hills the spirits hold

There, the cloudless sky, where twilight always seeps
Is deepened by a rippling black
And glowing mauve suspended at its edge
Reveals the surging fields below

Those dampened blue meadows imbued with green
Contain the secrets of this life
Of every thought and every word conceived
Between the Hills the spirits hold

With earthly eyes, I roam these hallowed plains
I trespass inside timelessness
I comb through treasures kept by someone else
But those same voices called me here

Returning now, I feel detached and changed
Untouched, yet like a sound, compressed
I shift with every blink, but seem so still
Just like these hills the spirits hold

Alone, I course the fields with fading hope
And wait for them to show themselves
Until I'm sure they've found another home
But then, I hear their whispers sweep

Their sighs, as stark as dawn upon the sea
Assail my soul. I run and hide
Afraid they'll disappear if I am seen
Within the hills the spirits hold

I listen under cover of the night
Unable to observe them, and yet near
I picture their whimsied resplendency
And hear their softened shining songs

In all its grace, they sing creation's tale
Of galaxies collapsed to dust
Of embers burnt eternal within stars
Of planets bound by swirling ice
Of oceans stilled reflecting skies above
Of mountains raised to conquer clouds
Of gilded pastures shimmering in the wind
And all that human hands have held

I long to be with them, to craft what has
No end. And that's when I'm sent back
Returning to myself, left only with
Ideas of where I must have been
I write a whisp of what I've found inside
The hills the spirits hold

Linda Ferguson

Emily Dickinson Was More Than a White Dress

Let them glimpse
a wisp
of angel's breath
and a dove's furtive,
shadowed flap—

Barefoot,
my vowels beat
a labyrinth
(a dance!)
between hemlock
maple, birch and beech—

It's not the house
I won't leave.
It's the forest
of my imagining—

Maria Illich

A wounded deer leaps the highest.

~ Emily Dickinson

Night Vision

Tonight, as the moon rides ripe and red above the crepe myrtles bordering the gardenias lining my backyard, I glance at the swimming pool, squeeze the St. Hubert medal hanging against my throat, and dive forty years down.

I'm a girl again, a restless preteen living in rural east Texas. It's midsummer, three hours past sundown. I ease the screen out of my bedroom window, drop behind Mom's oleander bushes, and inhale the musk of leaf and loam. Humidity slicks my skin. Everywhere, peepers flex their throats, blessing the night.

Crouching, I survey the backyard until I spot Begonia, our old bloodhound, lolling beneath the sweetgum tree. She twitches, as sleeping dogs do, probably dreaming of bones or hares or cool, deep holes. I bolt past her.

In the moonlight, I shine like virgin cotton.

Approaching the field of sorghum behind my house, I slow. Like a wader struggling against the surf, I push through the sorghum. Its coarse leaves brush my thighs with a sibilant hiss. Ahead, beyond a barbed wire fence, looms an old-growth stand of the piney woods. A dab of light bobs at its edge, like a corpse candle or will-o'-the-wisp. My heart quickens. It's Hunter, hanging his lantern from the dead hornbeam tree. With the lantern burning behind him, he stands cloaked in shadow and rimmed in light. Around him, the woods shift and murmur like the sea at low tide.

Hunter lives with his aunt, Miss Ruby, who grows fairy tale pumpkins, breeds harlequin rabbits, and writes letters to inmates. Dark of eye but light of spirit, Hunter knows these woods better than anyone. Where others see tangled thickets, he sees sassafras and sweet bay, scuppernongs and trumpet vine. He speaks sparrow, crow, and wren. Reads animal tracks and scat. Names bones.

We meet at the fence. Hunter pins the bottom strand of barbed wire to the ground with his boot and lifts the adjacent strand with his fingers.

I slip through the sudden space.

Hunter retrieves his lantern. With its glow, he locates the deer path leading to Holly Pond. We follow it, generations of leaves whispering beneath our boots.

Roughly heart-shaped and fed by a spring, Holly Pond attracts everything from armadillos to bobcats. Slender reeds and tall cattails frame its shallows, where bullfrogs thrum and tussle among the lotus pads. Everywhere, fireflies dazzle, then die.

An abandoned deer blind overlooks the pond. Hidden by honeysuckle (whose fragrance masks our scent), the blind is ideal for watching wildlife. I climb its weathered ladder, avoiding the creaky third rung. Hunter follows. Inside, we settle on a red cotton blanket and extinguish the lantern. Sheathed in shadow, we wait.

Below us, the pond reflects a full, claret moon, which slowly sinks behind an immense water oak thick with mistletoe. In the distance, a night bird calls. *Chuck-Will's-widow, Chuck-Will's-widow.*

I'm almost asleep when Hunter nudges me.

A white doe, bone pale, stands among the reeds and cattails. Lowers her head. Drinks.

Neither of us speak. We simply stare. Even after the doe bolts like white lightning down the deer path, we stare, our eyes watering as the shadows blur and spin like dark Catherine wheels.

Sometimes, the longer you look at something, the harder it is to see.

Hunter suddenly leaps from the deer blind. I scream. Landing in an awkward roll, he scrambles to his feet and races after the white doe. By the time I light the lantern and climb down the steps, both are gone.

In the days following Hunter's disappearance, Dad and Sheriff McPherson scour the fields and woods with two Texas Rangers and over ninety volunteers, some from as far away as Houston, while Mom consoles Miss Ruby with bundt cake and coffee. I recount my last night with Hunter multiple times, then cease speaking. Grief guts memory. Hunter's not coming back.

Tonight, all those half-forgotten faces blur into one as I focus on the moon, now risen high and bone bright. It's a lantern, left hanging from a dead hornbeam tree. I slip out of the pool. The chirring cicadas could be peepers blessing the night. And the shooting Perseids, fireflies, dazzlingly bright.

I could be that preteen again, bright as virgin cotton. Wading through the sorghum. Slipping through the barbed wire. Following a deer path to a heart-shaped pond where a white stag waits for a doe.

I could, finally, see.

Sharon Mitchell

Spirit Lake

The cedar-shingled store hunched
on the edge of the pebbled beach,
ringed by lodgepole pines.
Bright canoes lined the lake,
oblong beads stitched along the shore.

I remember the store's cool concrete
under my feet, eyes adjusting
to the sudden dark, the feeble
chirp of captured crickets.
Children darted in and out all day,
slamming the screen door,
swim trunk pockets full of fireballs
and Jolly Ranchers, ice cream
dripping down their wrists.

My family spent our summers
by the lakeshore. My brother swam.
My sister and I sunned and dozed,
always wondering what was
at the far end of the lake, beneath
its murky water and sharp pines,
ink-jabs against the sky.

One day we took a yellow canoe,
my sister and I, and paddled
to the distant shore. The hollow
bottom scraped a barren beach,
the water cold and still.

The store was too far,
a tiny postcard viewed through
binoculars the wrong way.

On a shoreline boulder sat a girl,
face hidden by a dark twist of hair.
When we called, she didn't answer.
We looked again, and she was gone.

Uneasy, we pushed our bright
canoe into the water, pulling oars
hard across the lake. We rowed
and watched the sun move
down the sky. Tree-shadows
reached long across the water,
the lake a giant sundial.

When we arrived, red lights flashed.
A crowd stood in the bait store lot.
On the ground lay a pair of legs
and yellow trunks—a boy we knew.
We knew.

That day is yellow, the scrape
of boat-bottom, lapping water,
a slamming door. Dark hair,
a dark lake, shadowed
by lodgepole pines.

Linda Ferguson

Love Poem

We live in the forest of our hearts—
nest of moss and fern and oak
woven with the heathered lilt
of hills and whiskey and peat fires.

By day we wing,
by night, like leaves,
we curl and tuck,
our limbs entwined.

Beneath, tweed of roots and earth,
above, fingers of Pacific firs
reach to comb honey
from moors of stars.

Jennifer Lagier

In the Mansion of Stars

Twilight hummingbirds
probe lavender blossoms,
draw sustenance from salvia,
explore scarlet tubular blooms
of rogue Christmas cactus.

Overhead, cosmic illumination
pricks evening's sapphire mantle.
Smoky rivulets of white fog
undulate between houses.
Lunar orb ascends, framed
by silvery branches.

I sprawl on brick steps,
sip herbal tea, sniff garden perfume,
give thanks for small blessings:
cooling relief, summer lilies,
nightfall's dignified calmness.

Sterling Warner

Beguiling

Between shadows and light where
fingers ring bells, hands beat drums,
and witches toss off gossamer gowns

to bask nude bodies beneath the moon,
I watched the ceremony an outsider,
hidden behind wild roses and golden oaks;

glancing at lithe arms reaching high above,
feet barely touching the earth below,
pagan, perhaps—immoral, not at all—just

a momentary reprieve from daylight activities
where they lose themselves in self-contained
worlds, seldom sharing—hardly conversing—

rarely appreciated by peers. When I stumble
into the clearing uninvited, esoteric priestesses
as uninhibited as sirens approach me from all sides,

summon my spirit like sylphish courtesans,
induce me to joining their sky clad dance,
at one with the night, revering the universe.

Kerfe Roig

Harvest Moon

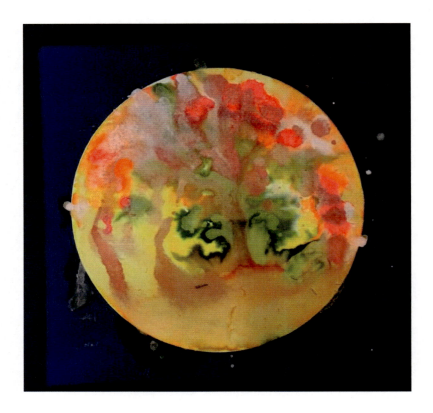

Krissi Stocks

On Assignment in Harbour Grace

I sigh, maneuvering my car between ruts in the highway where water has pooled. I am exhausted and cranky. It stormed all night, and our newborn, Iris, wouldn't go down. The last thing I am in the mood for is a filler story, something to keep the locals entertained. But here I am, an hour outside the city, to write a story about a circle of beech trees near Harbour Grace for the Gazette. Nothing grows between the trees. They say fairies gather there at night. I crack my window and inhale the sweet smell of spring, sunlight drying grass soaked by heavy rain.

I reel the car onto a soggy dirt path, lichen lining the trail. In the centre, there's a young girl, maybe six or seven, flagging me down.

As I pull up, I hear her shout, "You're here!"

I get out of the car. "Are you Tim's granddaughter? He said we'd meet at noon. I'm early."

She nods silently. She has eyes like nothing I've seen before: juniper-green. She's missing a front tooth and wearing a mossy tunic. Her unruly hair is poking out of her red-knitted-cap. I smile at her. Tim must've said she could go ahead.

"Come ON!" She says, "It's time!"

The girl pulls me with surprising force into the forest. We're running, flying over gnarled roots, spinning past green trees with fresh buds.

We land at what I assume is the fairy ring.

"This!" She says, cascading toward the ring of scraggly trees before she shuffles in, beckoning me with a single wave.

"Beautiful!" I say, trying to appease the girl. I'm a little uneasy. There's a sightless, soundless buzz in here I can't explain. My nerves feel the way your face does after the freezing wears off at the dentist. Tingling.

The girl traces her finger along a carving in the tree. It's the shape of a heart, but the edges are triangular, something a child would do.

"You carve this?" I ask.

The girl nods and laughs, a chortling, wheezy thing that makes her sound ninety-years-old.

I run my finger along the carving.

"Pretty." She says, pointing at the diamond necklace my fiancé gifted me for our anniversary.

"Oh," I say, touching its pendant.

She continues to stare.

"Would you like to try it on?"

She nods, beaming. I take the necklace off and wrap it around her neck, fumbling with the clasp.

"Oi!" I hear in the distance. It's Tim. "You're early!"

I look back to explain his granddaughter's showing me the fairy ring when I hear her cackle, playful and quick. I turn. She's gone. My hands are still midair where I was clasping the chain, but the necklace is gone. I frantically look up and down. *What the…?*

Tim reaches the ring, saying, "I said wait by the car!"

"Your granddaughter… took … She showed me her carving and…."

I point to the tree where the carving was. There's nothing there.

"My granddaughter? I don't…."

Tim looks perplexed for a moment – then realization melts his face, and he suddenly laughs.

"What did she take?"

"My anniversary necklace… What's happening?!"

Tim smiles and hands me a fistful of breadcrumbs.

"Put these in your pocket. There are faeries here."

Annie Snider

Observation

Small thin stalking mushrooms with white ink caps on,
drops of rain still clinging to the texture before sliding
to the damp, busy forest floor
where wet wood is broken like bread
and the past lives of seasons lie decomposing quietly.
These translucent fungi sprang up
just last night, and they look it: neonatal
and fragile as if a stiff wind could decapitate them
but until then, they dance in the gentle breeze,
reaching up, away from the spongy earth
Flecks of tiny bugs, microflora evidence of
their life prior to ascension
Nearby, angelwing leaves lift up off the ground
as if to say,
                Take me. Take me. Take me.

Charles Darnell

Mushrooms

Though you do not see
the brown spore
and tread uncaring
on the humus
that gives us birth,

while you lie sleeping,
and the pale moon bathes
our domed heads
with soft silver-white,
we grow,

we will live,
and we are silent
when you find us
in the morning light.

Victoria Dym

Fruitbody

Cynthia Bernard

Mycelia

Eucalyptus trees stand
in stark isolation—
mandated social distancing
to reduce fire danger.

A colony of fungi
work for wages around their roots,
taking their salary in carbohydrates,
captured sunlight.

The workers spin long threads,
mycelia, which connect to the fungi
of nearby trees and plants—
a cellular communication network.

How did it feel to the trees, then,
to have their neighbors
cut down, dug up, sliced,
and hauled away?

Was it like an amputation,
or like having a best friend
move far away
with no forwarding address?

Were they shocked?
Do they mourn?

Did they howl in outrage,
a silent mycelial scream?

Are they howling still?

Lorena Caputo

Roots

pure architecture

Jean Ryan

Lyme Ticks and Ladybugs

For nine to ten months each year the male bowerbirds of New Guinea work on their bowers. The style of the bower depends on the species. "Maypole" builders place hundreds of sticks around a sapling, winding up with a great mushroom-shaped structure. Other birds create "avenue" bowers, vertical rows of twigs imbedded in the earth between a narrow passageway. After construction, some of the more fastidious males will use their sharp beaks to paint the inside walls with plant juices. Finally, the birds begin to decorate, using whatever strikes their fancy: hunks of moss, red berries, silver snail shells, golden leaves, flowers, feathers, stones. Their whimsy extends even to manmade items: discarded batteries, toothbrushes, coins, nails, rifle shells, pieces of glass, strips of cellophane. Color is important. Some bowerbirds favor blue tones, while others prefer white or orange. Work is never quite finished; the birds spend weeks rearranging their treasures and adding to the plunder—stealing from one another is a common practice.

And the purpose of these sylvan palaces? It's the same old story: seduction. Year after year these indefatigable birds give everything they've got for the chance to spend a few glorious seconds on the back of a female. Rich in suitors, the female bowerbird flies from one endeavor to another, assessing and rejecting, till she finally lands on the threshold of the bower she likes best. Sometimes she obliges the waiting male right away; other times she requires coaxing, and the frenzied male will offer her gifts, a blue paperclip, an orange leaf. If these fail him, he will strut back and forth, extending his wings and chattering loudly so that she can see what a superb specimen he is. Many females end up selecting the same male and returning to him the next year, paring the chances for the other males whose efforts are nonetheless worthy.

So, what becomes of all the bowers that don't make the cut? Do they fall into disrepair, victims of time and weather? Or do the builders themselves do the dismantling, starting from scratch each fall, their bird brains brimming with fresh ideas?

I have no trouble believing that the initial impulse to build a bower is a reproductive imperative. At some point, though—perhaps after the forty-eighth golden leaf, the first dozen blue parrot feathers—I think this primal urge is forgotten and what drives the male after that is his own enthusiasm, craft turned to ecstasy. For what difference would it make to the no-nonsense, time-constrained female that there are thirteen parrot feathers instead of twelve, or that the interior, which she may not even bother to inspect, is freshly painted?

Only to the builder does every leaf and feather matter; each year, from fall through spring, nothing matters more. That his work may be in vain is something he is not prepared to ponder.

People, on the other hand, expect reward. The formulas we are taught — hard work equals success, healthy living ensures longevity, good deeds bring good luck — these ideas die hard and not without bitterness. Our house is blown away; the tumor is malignant; the dog we adopted gets hit by a car. "It's not fair," we cry; moreover, it doesn't make sense. Why would God allow such things?

Why are we sharing our home with polio and salmonella and brown recluse spiders? Where is the virtue in poisonous toadstools and powdery mildew? Indeed, our madcap inventor seems to have as much interest in the growth of a fungus as he does a fetus.

Whatever your religious views, one thing is certain: a long time ago this ball got rolling and a force we can't fathom gave it the nudge. From that point on, life never looked back.

 Consider the extravagance of species on this planet: one-hundred and forty kinds of sparrows, and every one of them changing, each generation bringing better beaks, designer tails, new come-hither stripes. So many versions of a small brown bird, all of them vying for a little more time. Why not, say, a dozen species? Wouldn't that be a sufficient sparrow allotment? Why is the earth burdening itself with this colossal balancing act?

Watching children play or dolphins leap or eagles soar, it's easy to conclude that life is fun, that we are put here to enjoy ourselves. Take male lions, which spend their days on grassy plains, dozing in the sun, dining on warm fresh prey, thanks to the prowess of their harems. Then take a look at male emperor penguins, which spend long winters on open ice, huddled together for warmth, risking starvation, a single precious egg balanced on their frigid feet. A tortoise trudges along for well over a century; a mayfly gets less than a day. One bird scores a mate with just a couple songs, while another must build a palace. Not one of these creatures knows the difference. "Why" is a question we might all do without.

To be born is to have worth. Lucky or not, lovely or not, everything on this busy blue orb gets a fighting chance to do its best. Rust and roses. Slugs and swans. Lyme ticks and ladybugs.

Does it feel good to be a ladybug? We can't say. All we can witness is the effort: one tiny being earning its life.

It hurts to be alive, too much and too often for pleasure to be the point; much of the time we manage without it. Now and again we are taken by surprise. In the oddest moments — spreading mulch, washing a plate, buttoning a child's coat — we are suddenly, inexplicably, happy. For the bowerbird, whose life amounts to little more than labor, the joy is built right in.

Karla Linn Merrifield

Organic Tanka

~après *Ralph Waldo Emerson*

A cricket's spirit
has a pure architecture
all its own. Her psalm
sounds through October's moon—
my understory lullaby.

Greg Illich

In a Fading Time

We count the days
as leaves falling
in a darkling wood

Angular shapes of cranberry, gold
and russet
covering the forest floor
pierced by
intermittent shafts of light

Fleeting glory,
a season of life:
a moment's prismatic gleam
in a drop of evening dew

Shy sunlight
disappears behind a brooding cloud

Faltering warmth
in a fading time
which shrouds a hope
we cannot entirely recall

Diaphanous, yet lambent
behind the thin veil of time

Twilight deepens at the forest's eaves
An evening breeze brushes our cheeks
stirs the leaves

A gentle murmur

A soft mist gathers about the trees
diffusing their dark boles
And we wait…

We hear
the mournful calls
of the whippoorwill,
and hold our breath
during the long silence
in between.

Ann Calandro

Before the Soup

Paul Gutting

Daylight Savings

January's cold is blowing in
The first snow of the year
Not the last of the season though

I don't know if we have enough
Holiday left from last month
To get us through the cold darkness

We may have to content ourselves
With timing the dawn until spring

Paul Gutting

D. C. al Fine

A rusted lake
Bleeds through duckweed into forest
Life stumbles through the muck
Nothing lush pastoral or romantic

About the stench
Rainbow fungus fetid muck rot
The deer do neither drink
Nor stand except by desperation

Alive with death
Bustling with decomposers
A generation's time
Will fill it in with meadow grass then grove

Assimilate!
Forest – claim this place – dig deep
Pond meadow grove forest
A changing life is an everlasting life

I will return
Body, soul reclaimed as ash — parts
Of new pieces, new lives
As generations gone are part of me

And will have left
Only these few broken
And boggy tracks to be
Then followed into forested time

Charles Darnell

Crysalis

There is an aphorism
that some things never change.

I am not sure.

As I look around me,
as I reflect on the long years
of my life,
the world is full
of transformation.
I gaze at the back
of my hand as I type
these very words,
the raised blue rivulets
of veins,
the skin creased,
wrinkles rippling with
stop and start as fingers fly
across keys.
In younger days,
these hands were smooth,
skin pink and fingers straight,
bent and scarred today.

I look out my window,
musing on words for this poem
and see a butterfly,
wings tattered now,
near the end of life.

It was only weeks ago,
a caterpillar slowed
its ravenous consumption
when time told it
change was demanded.
It found a safe place
away from the beaks of birds,
away from the careless
brush of my hands
in the garden,
spun itself into
a cocoon hardened by air.
Inside, a transformation
over mere days,
emergent wet wings
dried in the morning sun.

Man's changes are not so dramatic.
Years on years of slow
transmutation from infant
to old man hardly noticed
in the instant,
but profound in reflection.

Cynthia Bernard

Weathered Wood

When winter approaches,
once beflowered vines
will have endured summer's drought
and, desiccated, fallen to the earth below,
to be picked over by chattering birds
then trampled by sneakered feet
and an assortment of paws.

But there will have been a time, perhaps October,
an in-between, a twilight,
when the flowers have spent their loveliness
and their skeletons droop like deflated balloons,
when arthritic branches still trace their silhouettes
against tree trunks of weathered wood,
and weary roots, approaching their long hibernation,
still send sustenance up the xylem
and out to the branches.

Then, every so often,
a blossom will emerge
in solitary splendor —
penultimate offering,
the almost final verse.

reaching for the faun

M. C. Aster

Afternoon Lights

It begins with a rustle, a swirl, and a sough
that blows through an alley thick with leaves,
and small crinkly noises that might be sighs—
as if there's a faun on the loose.

Leaping in and out of the shadows, he pauses
to look; the dappled shade hides him. And then
he's off, sliding without a sound through a field
full of herbs, leaving behind a bent flower or
two, and a trail of perfumed scat.

Late in the day, he's prancing toward the dark
woods, hooves flashing silver and gold. And
in a green grotto, a woman sleeps in a nest
of crushed sage and trillium, her arm still
reaching for the faun that was.

Chelsea Grieve

dream of tir-na-nog*

catch me in a moment of fantasy
eyes glazed with magic
reflecting *tir-na-nog*

fields of heather glowing
in moonlight greeting hidden stream
trickling over ancient gems

catch me twirling on the surface
water as stage; stars as spotlight
tangled hair crowned with teacup roses and lilacs

trees stretching to clouds with knurled arms
forgetting secrets locked inside druid souls
witnessing dreams and destruction through weathered eyes

catch me with playmates flitting about
tasting the lust of escape on my tongue
turkish delight no longer available *only* in narnia

a sacred reverie possessed by the child
with a myriad of fantasies melding sunset into sunrise
harkening a day of possibility shadowed by reality

catch me drinking the freedom of sparkling wine
bare legs scratched and bloody from play
little trunks beneath a cotton gown

connecting me with dirt and vines
transforming into the willow trees
protecting our sweet *tir-na-nog*

please

catch me in a moment of fantasy
eyes glazed with magic
reflecting *tir-na-nog*

(*)An Irish legend of a paradise and supernatural realm of everlasting youth, beauty, health, abundance, and joy.

M. C. Aster

The Old Toll Bridge

It's an ancient bridge on a grassland's edge, boasting a small, weathered sign: "To cross—pay what you're able." Who built this span of huge timbers, now polished smooth by winds and time? No one knows. Its decking has grayed and yet every board stays perfect, without so much as a crack. There's also this: the bridge arcs over a laughable trickle of water that's barely five fingers wide and deep.

It's a snap to bypass the bridge and jump this wannabe brooklet—but only strangers to this county are fools enough to ignore the worn sign's ask. For there are eyewitness accounts of what happens if you try crossing without payment—a flashy Corvette and driver, a dozen Hell's Angels, and in days of yore, long before the "horseless carriage" arrived, entire wagon trains were known to disappear. One minute — they were right here. The next, they were not.

The folks in town don't dwell on their oddity much, but sometimes, when the last pot of coffee is gone, and the whiskey flows, talk turns to things people claim to have seen on the bridge. There's the three-headed dog that wears reading glasses on just one head, a yeti in a tutu that dances under each blue moon, and a ghostly girl atop a unicorn that's been seen on Halloween. Such tales bring smiles and laughter, but most folks agree—this bridge has an unknown master. Else how to explain the always artfully clipped trees in the nearby park—a park that wasn't built by either the state or the city, a park without a speck of litter? But for all the locals, tradition trumps mystery: folks take pride in using the bridge and paying a penny, a quarter, and a paper dollar works just fine, thank you. They drop the fee into a 103 slot that's been cut into a large oak timber, with a plaque above that simply says: IN.

These days there's not much new gossip, but on holiday nights people may gather in the town's cozy pub, and someone is sure to bring up some quite recent events. A year or two ago, a gaggle of kids dared each other to camp on the toll bridge overnight. But none could sleep a wink because of the loud growling and the sound of rattling chains from deep inside the pylons. Belatedly, the teens remembered to feed the slot with whatever change they had — and then they fled like scared rabbits. The pub's patrons began laughing and snickering because adults know that once you tickle that slot with some real American money, the growling changes into loud purring.

But Joe, the old publican, raised a finger to stop the levity. In somber tones, he reminded those present that the strange bridge of theirs had somehow been able to tell apart the town's naughty teens from all those out-of-town scofflaws that chose, of their own free will, to flout the bridge's very modest financial request. Further, he thought it's been a mistake not to show how much the town appreciated that the bridge didn't "disappear" any of the kids. After a moment or two, a councilman made an official motion, everyone voted in favor, and one of the cowboys sent his two-gallon hat around. It was full to the brim in very little time.

Next day, a small group of pub regulars — and a couple of town fathers who didn't want to be left out — drove to the bridge and fed an estimated two hundred dollars, coin by coin, into the usual slot. The publican left last; he whispered a few kind words and paid three shiny silver dollars — one for each of his grandkids that had camped on the bridge. He turned to go when the bridge began to shake and make popping sounds. It went on like that — shake, pop, shake, pop — for quite a while, when it dawned on him. That unusually large payment had given the bridge a case of hiccups! Feeling he ought to say something polite, all he could think of was "Gesundheit." For as far as he knew, there were no special greetings for a bridge in digestive distress. Grinning like the wild man he wasn't, Joe understood he'd just witnessed a new legend in the making. But to be on the safe side, he'd keep it on the QT. He was quite sure the bridge would like that.

Sharon Mitchell

The Naiad's Dream *

In a secret glade, forgotten,
rimmed with granite, slick and black,
water tumbles, sparkling
from a crystal mountain creek.

Rimmed with granite, slick and black,
the leaf-lit forest glimmers.
From a crystal mountain creek,
mist glazes moss and fern.

The leaf-lit forest glimmers,
somnolent with summer heat.
Mist glazes moss and fern
where they cling to ruins of stone.

Somnolent with summer heat,
water tumbles, sparkling,
clinging to ruins of stone
in a secret glade, forgotten.

(*) Naiad: a fresh water nymph in Greek Mythology

M. C. Aster

The Mavka at Midnight*

The moon's pale disk falls into the pond, and
The waterlilies catch it. They sail on together —
A floral lamp adrift on the water.

A sudden upswell — call her water sprite, nymph, or
Mavka — reveals the lake's keeper and mistress.
The mavka notes the moon's distress, and
Nudges the lilies to release their captive.

Black hair dripping, the nymph climbs ashore —
A breathless marble goddess resting in the ferns.
A fox arrives to lap the cool water, but the mavka
Can't help it; she impishly flicks beads of water
Into the air. Startled, the fox disappears with
A swish of her white-tipped tail. The mavka
Sighs — and for a while she just paddles
In the moon's jade-and-silver wake.

But it's a slow summer night, without a single human
Intruder for the restless mavka to drown. The cricket
And frog serenade is nice but lacking. She takes
One very small breath — and dives under the reeds
Until tomorrow's moonlight wakes her.

(*) *Mavka: Ukrainian nymph and minor water deity with a trickster's inclinations.*

Wendy Dunmeyer

Eridanus*

Hovering over a virgin marsh,
        hawks shift shadows
in midwinter twilight.

Falling snow bows rushes fleeced by wind,
        frosts shoreline rocks
from onyx to moonstone

soon lustered by moonlight and heaven's
        sweet-water river,
the ancient path for souls.

(*) The constellation Eridanaus, thought of as a sacred river, begins at the foot of Orion & winds its way southward to its brightest star, Achernar. It is associated with the Greek myth concerning the rise and fall of Phaeton.

Wendy Dunmeyer

selene, to pandia*

come, daughter, twilight fades,
and you must prepare
for love

come, bathe in oceanos,
and robe your limbs
with clouds

blushed by sun's diffusing
light; rinse your flowing,
silver tresses

in nightglow; ribbon aurorae
through your curls, trailing
one stray

tendril over your shoulder;
dust your eyes dusk,
your cheeks

mother of pearl; circle
your wrist and neck
with long,

loose strands of moonstones;
mist evening primrose across
your décolleté—

then, like a mist,
rise up through this
silent world,

find your chosen one,
and as he sleeps,
kiss him

with your stainless light—
he will follow wherever
you lead

as lesser stars fade
out of sight

(*) Pandia: daughter of the sky-god Zeus and the moon-goddess Selene in Greek mythology.

Paul Gutting

Calling the Wild

A shady satyr beckons
Leaning from a cruelty of shadows
Between buildings

He pulls a fedora over his horns
And glances up the street
Lifting his tweedy lapel

The pipes dangle
Almost alluringly
Between his furred nipples

Pipes of promise
Pipes of hope
Pipes to play shade into sunlight

The blood tingles with temptation
But who has the price of reprieve
Whose pocket holds

The desirably tiger exotic
When all you can own or carry is
The plainly sparrow ordinary

Instead, you take snickering initiative
Seeking to draw the pipes
You dance the heat of your blood — shouting

"Play rose petal butterflies
Into my cathartic fire!
I will dance through their ashes!"

He cannot but play for your feet and hips
Pounding and swaying in the open
To the brink of collapse

Clicking cloven time marks his brazen steps
He draws his breathy lips
To your ear to whisper

"Lay down your symbols. Speak plain.
For the world can only give
What you ask of it.

You seek reprieve?
Here is forgiveness.
Seek no more."

He takes your sweaty head in both hands
Pulls it to his lips and leaves you
Trembling in the sun

new voltaires

Ann Howells

Welcome Morning

Dove, like wind-bowed reeds,
peck scattered seed
while a three-quarter moon
reverts to lace.
Sparrows twitter gossip;
grackles like arrogant test pilots
strive to break the sound barrier.
Every unfurled leaf glistens
as though beaded in glass,
and the heavy-lidded owl,
belly replete,
returns to his oak.
A wheelbarrow,
pavéd in dew, reclines.
Ebullient light spills over
a pastel palette,
heralds muscular blue skies,
fresh promise, opportunity.

Ann Howells

Day of the Dragonflies

Beneath the maple –
dragonflies engage in mating ritual,
orgy of spring, celebration of fecundity.

Unaware, my terrier circumvents the lawn,
seemingly not entirely familiar
though he has marked every fencepost, downspout,
and raised tree root.

But I,
coffee cup stilled halfway to my lips,
am enchanted –
errant sparks flash electric blue, chromium green
like glitter within a shaken waterglobe,
translucent shimmer of silver-edged wings
reminiscent of old etchings: Pandora's box thrown open,
man's tribulations surging to gyre and whorl.

And I wonder if this might be the antithesis:
a constellation of delights
                to assuage a troubled mind.

Kendra Preston Leonard

Replenish

Save the seeds from your own plant
if they've thrived in your garden —
they'll be better than the ones that come in the mail,
through heat or cold or wet,
huddled together in their little packets.

Plant something rare, plant a crop of
things you've never seen or eaten before,
plant rivers of seeds,
make seed banks, and let your neighbors withdraw.

Old seeds aren't ready for the present day;
they were taught to thrive in a different climate,
in different soils
plant them anyway and see what happens.
Plant the new beside them
and replenish;
make your garden grow,
oh new voltaires.

Mobi Warren

Diadasia Bee Asleep in a White Prickly Poppy

Alice Campbell Romano

It Never Rains in Los Angeles

Rain blew in from the West last night
like an old friend
I hardly expected to see again.
I was slipping into sleep
when drops rattled my window
but instead of rousing me
the wet outside found my skin.
I turned on my side,
crossed my legs, and they
were round and soft again
and my arms were no longer thin
and I fell asleep, and this morning
the sun is out as it always is
but I am still ripe and filled
in my remembered body.

Chris Billings

Skinny Dipping

wade in
up past the ankles
to the knees
feel the water lap rhythmically
against shins
kneecaps
knees bend slightly
hands break the surface
toes push off gently
head underwater
body glides effortlessly
no wet clothes
dragging
no swimsuit
clinging
the healing water
streams by
massaging every inch
of bare skin
feeling exposed
yet comforted
the water hugs
like amniotic fluid hugs
offering protection
the freedom
of being naked and vulnerable
up for breath
back under
in a welcome embrace
washing pressures away

soothing a hard life lived
glide with ease
roll over
back float
face up to the sky
then underwater again
back toward shore
stand reluctantly
water sliding
dripping
off bare skin
splashing the surface
walk slowly to shore
gradually leaving
her comforting embrace
feeling clean
fresh
newborn

Alice Campbell Romano

Gods of a Hudson River Storm

I stop unwise under an oak for the August storm
that will soon sweep over the river and into the trees,

its annunciation the air, alive, warm, thick on my skin.
I am only seven, spellbound by anticipation. The breeze

begins its whisshhh-whisshhh in the high oak leaves
and the sky comes closer, dark like a tarnished platter,

slashed by bright, bare branches of lightning
before clouds crash together and wind fills the woods

with possibilities, and then the rain starts, drops
like glass teardrops, far apart, then faster, faster

until a gray wall moves across the river and soaks
everything, makes ferny air rise up rich with wet dirt

and new oxygen, so I know these woods, these trees,
are where the real gods live, and I shout through

crashing thunder, tell the thunder and the rain
and the wind I know what you are. I am you.

Chris Billings

The Nelipot Way

Tread softly with bare feet
upon earth mother's brow
she will teach you to mind your step
watch the path ahead
be awake, take your time
she will energize you
fill you with an awareness of your surroundings
that the shod will never know

Stand easy but firmly on her bosom
toes grasping gently her mother's skin
feel the grains of sand beneath your feet
blades of grass tickling your soles
soft mud cool and squishy
she will reward you
with songs and stories of life
if you but listen to her vibrations

Cleanse your feet in her healing waters
ocean tides, lakes lapping the shore
easy flowing creeks and streams
refresh your spirit from hard city sidewalks
feel the shifting sands beneath your feet
she will calm your soul
with her soothing motion, the pulsing
of her constant ebb & flow

Wander easily with feet unshod
saunter with slow deliberate abandon
upon her rough, delicate surface
feel the pulse of her life-force with each step
honor her and she will give you joy
she will give you life, if you simply
tread softly with bare feet
upon earth mother's brow

Spirit Thom

14 Ways to Stay Awake

KEEP YOUR EYES & EARS OPEN @ ALL TIMES
Be alert, alive, aware in every moment.
Attuned to all, each, every person you meet.
Even in dream state, remember your dreams.
Seek answers in them.
We are all @various levels of awareness.
Listen Deepen and dredge!
Seek core truths-paradigms unlocking paradoxes.
Look for diamond eyes that shine-
Smiles that share awareness.
Parables beyond desk calendar cliches. Read all
Masters, Mistresses, Fools
Seek the oral and the aural.
Resonate with landscapes & elementals.
Sleep when you are dreaming
and dream while you are awake.
Someone somewhere has already shared
these modes and strategies.
There are always more. But you only asked for 14.

Biographies

Alex Angeline writes to realize the impact of love, death, nature, and life. Her remarkable mother instilled in her the courage to share those words as art. She is grateful to live with her inspiring wife, Hannah, and their sage and dog, June, in their sunny home in California. She runs a fulfilling business with Hannah centered around diversity and inclusion. She has a BS in business from Miami University and is slowly pursuing her MDiv at Claremont School of Theology. Her work can be found in *Minerva Rising's, The Keeping Room* or on Instagram @alexangelinewrites.

M. C. Aster was born in Yugoslavia, lived in Ethiopia as a child, and worked in several European countries. Aster's diverse background and interest in nature, history, and folklore influence her writing. Publications include: *Phantom Drift, Meat-for-Tea, Borrowed Solace, WayWords, Star82-Review* and many others. Her work is forthcoming in *Painted Bride Quarterly*. A Pushcart Prize nominee, Aster lives in Southern California and fosters two endangered Mojave Desert tortoises.

Cynthia Bernard is a woman in her late sixties who is finding her voice as a poet after many decades of silence. A long-time classroom teacher and a spiritual mentor, she lives and writes on a hill overlooking the ocean about twenty miles south of San Francisco.

Chris Billings is a member of the Maverick Poets in San Antonio. His poems have been included in several anthologies and he has independently published five chapbooks of poetry. He currently lives in Schertz, TX.

Lynne Burnett's poems have appeared in many magazines and anthologies, and she was a finalist for the Montreal International Poetry Prize 2022. Her muse is "Santosha": complete contentment — both an attitude and state of deep inner peace.

Ann Calandro is a writer, artist, and classical piano student. Her short stories have been published in *The Vincent Brothers Review, Gargoyle, Lit Camp, The Fabulist,* and *The Plentitudes*. She is the author of the poetry chapbook *Verbal Silences* (Duck Lake Books 2020) and of three illustrated children's books (Shanti Arts). Find more: www.anncalandro.webs.com .

Before the Soup, 20 X 16" collage (2014): considered *enchanted realism*, it is composed of photographs I took and shows the prelude to cooking and eating a bowl of vegetable soup: a woman is searching, basket on her arm, for various kinds of vegetables in a magical forest where the vegetables grow combined on trees and thinking about what kind of soup to cook and eat. I make collages with paper, colored pencil, marker, pastel, paint, chalk, and photographs that I take. I also draw with wet and dry pastels. My art style is realism, but there's something askew about it. I call it *enchanted realism*, located at the four-way intersection of reality, dreams, wishes, and memories. I often incorporate words and musical terms, notes, or instruments into my artwork.

Lorraine Caputo is a wandering troubadour whose poetry appears in over 300 journals on six continents, and 20 collections of poetry – including *Notes from the Patagonia* (dancing girl press, 2017), *On Galápagos Shores* (dancing girl press, 2019) and *Caribbean Interludes* (Origami Poems Project, 2022). She also authors travel narratives, articles, and guidebooks. Her writing has been honored by the Parliamentary Poet Laureate of Canada (2011) and nominated for the Best of the Net. Caputo has done literary readings from Alaska to the Patagonia. She journeys through Latin America with her faithful knapsack Rocinante, listening to the voices of the *pueblos* and Earth. Follow her adventures at www.facebook.com/lorrainecaputo.wanderer or https://latinamericawanderer.wordpress.com.

Artist Statement: Drawing, for me, is a meditation. I start with no preconception, no plans. I connect with my self / Self and allow it to lead the pen where it will go. Sometimes the interpretation of a work even escapes my conscious mind — the drawings can come from someplace so deep within — or even, perhaps, from some other dimension. These drawings are pen & ink on paper & 18.5 cmx 12.5 cm. Each drawing can take several days or even several weeks to complete.

Wendy Taylor Carlisle lives and writes in the Arkansas Ozarks. She is the author of four books and five chapbooks, and is the 2020 winner of the Phillip H. McMath Post-Publication Award for *The Mercy of Traffic*. Doubleback Books reprinted her 2008 book, *Discount Fireworks*, as a free download: https://tinyurl.com/FireworksCarlisle Find more: www.wendytaylorcarlisle.com.

Maryangel Chapman's work has appeared in several publications, and she would love to get paid for her writing one day.

Brigid Cooley (she/her) is a poet, journalist and storyteller based in Georgetown, Texas. She is dedicated to highlighting the stories of others, while also carving out a space to share her own experiences. She previously served as co-host for the Sun Poets Society's weekly poetry readings in San Antonio, and currently hosts virtual readings on the *Little Things Poetry Read* Facebook page. Her work has been published in several Texas based publications, including the Central Texas Writers Society's *Light and Darkness* anthology and the *skin* edition of the fws: international journal of literature & art.

Julieta Corpus left her belly button buried in a lot haunted by a woman dressed in white. Her work has appeared in *Texas Poetry Calendar* and in *Texas Highways*.

Victoria Costello lives and writes alongside oaks and pines in Southern Oregon. Her debut novel, *Orchid Child*, arrives in June of 2023 from Between the Lines Publishing. See more of her work at http://victoriacostelloauthor.com and follow her https://twitter.com/VCostelloAuthor

Susan Coultrap-McQuin is a retired educator, nature lover, and curious traveler. Recent poems have appeared in *Lowestoft Chronicle*, *Still Point Arts Quarterly*, *The Poeming Pigeon*, and *The Dewdrop* and in anthologies including *Capsule Stories Isolation Edition*, *This Was 2020*, *Quiet Diamonds* and *Made of Rust and Glass*. Her first chapbook, *What We Bring Home* (The Poetry Box), was released in October 2021. She has earned several awards for her poems, including being a finalist in the Orchard Street Poetry Contest and an Honorable Mention from Wick Poetry Center. Find her on Facebook and Twitter (@scoultra) and in readings on Youtube.

Charles Darnell is a poet living in San Antonio, Tx. He writes with the haphazard manner of a disorganized curmudgeon. His book of poetry, *Toward Human*, was published by Kallisto Gaia Press in May 2022.

RC deWinter's poetry is widely anthologized, notably in *New York City Haiku* (NY Times, 2017), *Now We Heal: An Anthology of Hope* (Wellworth Publishing, 2020) *easing the edges: a collection of everyday miracles* (Friends of the Boerne Public Library, 2021) and *The Connecticut Shakespeare Festival Anthology* (River Bend Bookshop Press, 2021). Her work appears in print in *2River, Event Magazine, Gargoyle Magazine, Meat For Tea: The Valley Review, the Minnesota Review, Night Picnic Journal, Plainsongs, Prairie Schooner, Ogham Stone, San Antonio Review, Southword, Twelve Mile Review, Variant Literature, Yellow Arrow Journal, The York Literary Review,* and in various online journals.

Wendy Dunmeyer loves poetry, wildflowers, and watercolor painting. Her poetry has been selected as a finalist for the Morton Marr Poetry Prize (2011) and honorable mention in NDSU's Poetry of the Plains and Prairies Chapbook Contest (2022) and has been published in *Measure, Natural Bridge, The Oklahoma Review*, and elsewhere. Her full-length collection, *My Grandmother's Last Letter*, is forthcoming from Lamar University Literary Press. To encourage future generations of poetry lovers and young poets, she has taught poetry classes for children at her local library and volunteered as a visiting writer for National Poetry Month at local elementary schools.

Victoria Dym has degrees in Clowning, Philosophy and Creative Writing, and is certified to teach Laughter Yoga. Her most recent book, *Spontaneous*, is available on Amazon. https://www.amazon.com/Spontaneous-Victoria-Dym/dp/B09VWMZMDT

Artist's Statement: The important, most nutritious part of the mushroom is the mycelium, hidden underground. What shows is the fruitbody, the bloom of darkness.

Linda Ferguson is an award-winning writer of poetry, fiction, and essays. She's also an amateur dancer who loves to draw, paint, and shoot the breeze.

Tristan Franz is a writer and educator from Brooklyn, New York. He writes mainly poetry and creative non-fiction and is interested in topics such as decolonial thought, cultural ecology and indigenous poetics. He holds an interdisciplinary master's degree in the study of the Americas from The City College of New York. You can find recent work at https://linktr.ee/tristanfranz

Chelsea Grieve is a Michigander, now living in the Sonoran Desert. She has published a few pieces, mostly creative nonfiction. She works in behavioral health and writes in her free time.

Paul Gutting has been a writer, artist, craftsman, and educator for many years. He has taught all ages from toddlers to adults, and currently works with incarcerated offenders. When not writing or teaching, he is often found in a crowded garden or a messy workshop. As a life-long writer in many genres, he won a Kevin Kline award in 2006 for Best Original Script.

Stephanie L. Harper is a proud mom of two extraordinary humans and a widely published poet who lives in Indiana with the world's most adorable husband and cat. Find her on Twitter @stephanielharp1 and on her website: slharperpoetry.com

Ann Howells edited *Illya's Honey* journal for eighteen years. She is a reluctant submitter, preferring to write (or do anything else) rather than submit.

Gregory Illich is a Public Affairs Officer for the Texas State Guard, a Tai Chi teacher, and a massage therapist. He enjoys poetry, drawing, and aviation.

Maria Illich is an author and educator whose dream job is wrangling jackalopes.

Bernard Jacobson is a previously unpublished poet aspiring to become the exact opposite.

Jennifer Lagier lives near the Pacific Ocean with two spoiled rescue dogs. She hikes wetlands, forests, beaches.

Kendra Preston Leonard writes spells, loves her garden's anoles, and wants to cuddle with the rabbit in the moon. She's published lots of poems.

Joan Leotta steps into the woods to gather pinecones, stories, leaves — and is sometimes joyfully surprised by encounters with birds and wood sprites. She was nominated for a Pushcart in both 2021 and 2022 and for the Best of Net in 2021. Her chapbook, ***Feathers on Stone"*** is forthcoming from Main Street Rag 2023 at https://tinyurl.com/LeottaPoems

Julie Martin, poet and a public-school teacher, lives near the confluence of the Mississippi and Minnesota Rivers. Find more of her work here: Sphinxmothrising.blogspot.com

Ruth McArthur's favorite pastime is looking out the window. Her poems have appeared in various small journals. Her chapbook, *Persistence*, is available through Finishing Line Press.

Karla Linn Merrifield, a nine-time Pushcart-Prize nominee and National Park Artist-in-Residence, has had 1000+ poems appear in dozens of journals and anthologies. She has 15 books to her credit. Her newest full-length poetry book, *My Body the Guitar,* from Before Your Quiet Eyes Holograph Series (December 2021), was nominated for the 2022 National Book Awards. Visit her website: https://karlalinnmerrifield.org/ & sign up for her blog here: https://karlalinnmerrifeld.wordpress.com/

Sharon Wright Mitchell is a neurodivergent teacher and poet. She studied literature and education at the University of Georgia. She has been published in *The American Journal of Poetry, The Wild Word,* and *FATHOM,* among others. Ms. Mitchell is a Georgia native and enjoys hiking the Appalachian foothills. For poetry and adventures, follow her on Instagram: @apoetseyeview

Robert Okaji no longer lives in Texas. His writing has appeared in over 200 literary journals/anthologies, which he finds difficult to believe.

Kerfe Roig is a resident of New York City who enjoys transforming words and images into something new.

Artist's Statement: The circle is a perfect vessel for watercolor and the natural world.

Alice Campbell Romano lived 13 years in Rome, Italy, turning Italian screenplays into American movie scripts. She worked with, among other superheroes, Federico Fellini. Honing dialog is good practice for a poet- —

encourages concision with character. Alice married an Italian; they raised their family in Rome and in Los Angeles. Alice is a published and anthologized poet whose work has just or will soon appear in, among others, *Prometheus Dreaming, Orchards Poetry, Quartet, David St John Anthology, Persimmon Tree, New Croton Review, Beyond Words, Writing in a Woman's Voice,* & *Pink Panther Magazine*. Alice's birthplace was in the Hudson Highlands. She is an active member of The Hudson Valley Writers' Center and so is home again—although Italy never leaves her heart and mind.

Jean Ryan lives in coastal Alabama and thinks retirement is highly underrated. She is the author of four books, including a collection of nature essays. Find more here: https://jean-ryan.com/

Annie Snider is a poet, collage artist with found objects, and an Artist in the Schools in San Antonio, TX. Instagram: @Anniesartish

Leslie D. Soule is a lover of trees, which is why she wrote this piece. Someday she hopes to pull a mysterious sword from a tree, like Sigurd the Volsung.

M. Lynne Squires, Pushcart Prize-nominated author, has penned 4 books and has had work included in anthologies and journals. She writes with her cats, Scout, and Boo Radley.

Krissi Stocks is a writer from Newfoundland, Canada.

Sandi Stromberg led a nomadic life until she arrived in Houston, where putting down roots in gumbo earth has been challenging. Yet, her nature thrives in her neighborhood. Coyotes amble, hawks hunt, blue jays feather nests.

Sterling Warner is an award-winning author, poet, & educator who enjoys writing, fishing, hosting virtual readings—and retirement. Widely published, his poetry collections include *Serpents Tooth* and *Flytraps* (2022).

Mobi Warren is a poet, naturalist, and puppeteer with a special affinity for native bees.

Artist's Statement: Discovering a sleeping bee clinging to a poppy's stamen is one of my sweetest finds ever and made me wonder what a bee might dream.

Liam Wilson's paintings have appeared as cover art for *the after: poems only a planet could love* by Terry Dawson, in Harvard-based *Liminal Spaces Art*, in *Beyond Words Literary Magazine,* and forthcoming in the Princeton based art and literary journal *Eco-Theo*. He has exhibited in Austin, Texas. Find him on Instagram at @bouringpaintings.

Melissa Wold is allowed to live with two rat terriers and currently writes for *Writers In Nature* through Mobile Botanical Gardens.

Spirit Thom is an improvising free verse Bard who plays with WORDJAZZ LOWSTARS . Thom is the Beat Poet Laureate of Texas 2020-2022/ He can best be seen improvising at Open Mics in Austin, Georgetown, Round Rock and elsewhere.

Jenny Wrenn is a dedicated writer in the borderlands of SE Arizona who has written a gazillion poems and published a few. Still, she writes. She can't help it.

Cynthia Yatchman (cover art) is a Seattle based artist and art instructor. She shows extensively in the Pacific Northwest. Past shows have included Seattle University, the Tacoma and Seattle Convention Centers and the Pacific Science Center.

Artist's Statement: I primarily use acrylic paint, latex paints, inks, papers, and charcoal. My images contain many diverse layers of meaning, from the universal to the specific and personal. Many of my works are abstract. I am frequently interested in pattern and/or creating a rich sensual surface by making layer upon layer of marks

Made in United States
Orlando, FL
11 December 2022